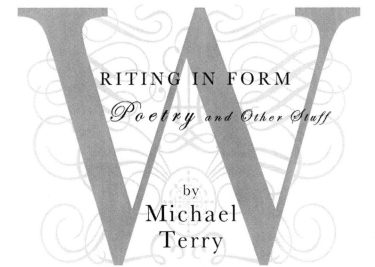

RITING IN FORM
Poetry and *Other Stuff*

by
Michael
Terry

COLD RIVER STUDIO
NASHVILLE, TENNESSEE

Cold River Studio is an independent press committed to introducing fresh, exciting voices to the reading public. It is our mission to take a chance on deserving authors and achieve the highest quality when bringing their words to the marketplace. We believe in the power of words and ideas and strive to introduce readers to new, creative writers.

Published by Cold River Studio, Nashville, Tennessee

First Edition: December 2009

Printed in the United States of America
ISBN 978-0-9842298-1-9

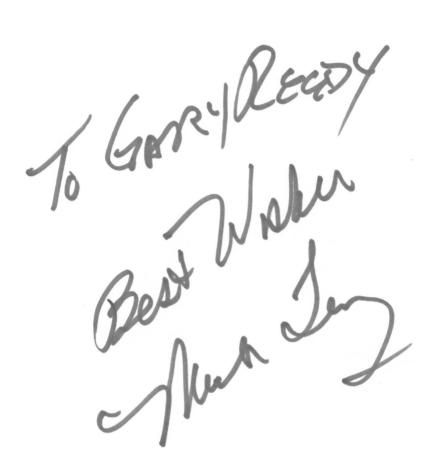

To Garry Reedy

Best Wishes

Mark Terry

DEDICATION

To my family for patience, kindness, and love.

*To Bryce Lambert for his dignity, wit and caring
that others could come to love language as much as he.*

TABLE OF CONTENTS

Working in Form　1

What's Art?　3

Gone Feral　6

Dresden　7

I Forgave　9

A Leg from Shankill　10

A Poem Should Have an Icy Scene　12

After Sex　16

The Baffled Bear　17

Apostate Tree　19

A Tornado Hit the Neighboring Town　22

The Life and Death of Russell and Me　32

Dropping Dirt　33

A New Tool　34

A Wolf and Me　35

My Mom Said No　38

Seeing Again　40

He Looked Like My Grandfather　41

Still in Love with You　44

Winter Can Be Pardoned　51

Tock, Tick　52

Random　53

Learning Relevance　54

Art From Life   57

You Catching Life's Woozle   60

You Must Suffer and Die Like Them   63

Dimensioning Orion   65

A Letter to My Red Maple   67

Blood Lines   71

In a Field of Clover   73

Growing Back   80

The Streets of Hell   81

A Casket, a Basket   82

Talk, Talk, Talk   84

Getting Exercise   85

Singles   86

One Sunny Day   88

I Wish People Had Tails Like Dogs   90

An Upset Woman in Normal Time   92

Certificate Demanded   94

Such Grudge   95

Limbo: The Fall   97

Redemption   99

My Memory Has Transformed You Into a Classic Beauty   100

Emmett Till Was a Catholic   102

Serious Radio   103

My Daughter Went to Bore-dink School   104

Long Division   105

The Rhyme is the Crime   106

Henotheism   109

I Know Not What I Knew   110

Pacing Time   112

Science Fails Again   113

Readers' Notes   115

We shall not cease from exploration,
and the end of all our exploring will be to arrive where we started
and know the place for the first time.
—T. S. Eliot

WRITING IN FORM

——■——

She was crabby, blabby and flabby . . . .

A motion picture is, a message is,
A mural is, a moral is

Is an image always an idea?
Is an idea always a representation?.

A photo is a portrait. Or not.
Real or fake: portrait or photo?

The delivery is only a device,
Less etched *in the mind* than *through the mind.*

Temporary and permanent both.

Hamlet may have had problems, but so did Eliot.
If I understand you, have you failed?

If a poem falls in the forest,
Will you be able to mix paint with words?

Letters are pictographs,
Characters are petroglyphs.

Semaphore is symbol.
I cannot talk, I lost my flags.

When the Indians smoke signals broke,
They used tom-toms.

To Macleish, the most important thing about a library
        is that it exists.
Like the words in libraries, derivative declarations
        may be mortal.

The poet's Archimedian tools lever his
Creation: a new (and personal) universe.

Complex and simple, both.

And a reader, a receiver, a consumer,
Tabula rasa, mensa rasa, mens rasa,

On whom the poet has his way,
Driving through the mind

A kind of cause and effect, both.

WHAT'S ART?

———■———

Exhausted, I sat down.
Sir!
That (very valuable) Chair is part of the exhibition!
Uh, sorry.
I walked into another hall.

Sir! Didn't you see the sign?
Uh, yeah, I thought the sign was part of The Exhibition.
Please, can't you see that the sign says Keep Out.
Yeah, but then the chair said Sit Down On Me.
In my mind it did, anyway.

I saw Fire Blazing in a Corner,
And I thought it was part of the exhibition.
And the Fire Extinguisher,
And the Wall-Mounted Alarm.
Not art?

I came to believe
My sensibilities were part of The Exhibition.
My observations and reflections, too.
Integrated and absorbed.
All is art and art is all.

No Cartesian radical doubter I,
Cogito and all that stuff.
The Fire,
The Device,
Me,

Distressing challenges to the aesthetic consciousness
Of every dilettante who alleges depth,
            crows his breadth and erudition,
Only to be discovered a Philistine.
The flame that sears your skin is real enough.
To you always, to me perhaps.

A revealing: the Emperor's New clothes, the Wizard of Oz.

Thus, skin unburned, no pain,
I learned that fire is art, only art.
The gallery, without insurance,
Burned to the ground.
It was a great exhibition.

I t is an artists' responsibility to be engaged with culture. And when the culture is going through turmoil, an artist can't ignore that. Not every artist has to be politically engaged, but I can't imagine that you can be an active participant of this culture and not in some way reflect that in the work you are creating.

—Lynn Nottage

GONE FERAL

—■—

Small birds, mammals and reptiles have gone feral.
Hamsters, guinea pigs, gerbils: gone feral, too.
White mice have revolted,
Parakeets refuse to be cute,
Crested cockatoos kill.
Domestic animals and pets, lab animals
Now bite, scratch, escape, defy,
Never to return as man's chattel.
Horses, cattle, sheep and goats rebel.
All animals are chaos;
Gone feral.
Only humans can now serve man's needs:
Clothing, food, transportation, companionship,
And medical testing.
And now, I have gone feral, too.

DRESDEN

———■———

The German spoke of Dresden through an old scarred face.
As he talked, I stared—impolite, no, rude—
Inaudible gasping.
His face and hands: scars, competing with wrinkles of age,
Yet together a duet, an orchestra:
A score of valleys and craters,
Interrupted by small plains, ridges and creases.

The horror of his face at first a metaphor
       for the horror of the place
Where he watched, as a small boy, his parents,
Blown to a few large chunks of meat,
Bits of clothing still clinging to what were,
       a moment before, people:
His mother and father.
And his sister, before his eyes,
       black and charred by the searing fire.
Hell.

Dresden, no icon for the pain, the torture of hell,
But hell itself.
Hell manufactured in the paradoxical pursuit of peace.
A thousand bombers, eight million pounds of steel
       doves on death wings,

Diving heavy to earth,
      freed by men flying metal machines of madness,
Keenly designed to marry science and gravity,
Delivering death to the ground so far below the screams,
      the collective agony, were but abstracts.

No pilot saw the small German girl set afire, run screaming,
Consumed,
Smelling of grilled meat,
Later that girl to have a different smell,
Her flesh not so burned as to turn to dust,
Enough flesh remaining unburnt to rot, putrefy.
The blackened and putrefied little girl of Dresden.

A withered British pilot whispered:
      "I remember . . .
      I flew in the last wave of bombers,
      Straight over Dortmund and Leipzig
      Through the German night sky.
      I was scared.
      A huge glow hung on the sky.
      Then, I could feel the heat;
      Great bloody site that was,
      Dresden afire.
      I loved it."

I FORGAVE

———■———

I forgave. I forgive.
There was nothing else to do,
But eat a bit of my own flesh each day.
Not chained like Prometheus,
No eagle arriving daily;
Only me in agony to consume myself
In an eternal enterprise;
Eating.
Pounding pain and suffering.
More eating.
Torture.
I should have eaten him or her or you.
Yet I ate myself in little bits.
Then I learned to forgive.
And then, I forgave.

A LEG FROM SHANKILL

———■———

I have a leg from Shankill,
An arm from the Bogside Battle.
From the Birmingham Pub, I've got a finger,
Still attached to a piece of hand.
Half an ear, blown from the side of a head
In Claudy, County Londonderry.
(Or is it Derry?)

I have a piece of brain, a scrap, a spoonful only,
Rent perhaps from a head
That had never considered that its fate
Was to be shredded by bullets fired,
Bombs laid by men hating other men,
Men who looked and thought just like each other,
Except for the mutual hate, that is.

I keep these precious pieces in jars of formaldehyde,
Sealed tight and labeled,
Stored safe in a small dark place.

I remove them from time to time . . .
Jars set upon my kitchen counter,

Me,
On a stool,
Staring at the bits and shards,
Lest I forget.

A Book of Poetry Should Have an Icy Scene

———■———

A book of poetry should have an icy scene;
Like winter, dark, I mean, fingers burn with the cold,
Bleak and drear, they told me so.

Evoke a shroud,
Thoughts laid lean and bare,
An eviscerating numbness.

They said my work had a positive tone
Which, not changed . . .
Why, you'll not get reviewed, pursued, construed.

You'll not be taken seriously
If you write of love and wind that crawls to freedom,
Finches, freesia, fitness.

Numb.
Career over,
Poetry done.

Critics render chaos.
Meter and stress,
Stanzas wrong, lines too long (like this one is when I add
          the parenthetical remark . . . it just gets ridiculous!)

AABAs and ABABs
Self-defile, earn enmity.
Write despair, death, gloom.
(Vachel Lindsay and Robert Service are forgot.)

Sure, some words are hot, not icy,
Nevertheless,
It goes like this:

> *Crows and ravens gather at the grave of your mother.*
> *Birds not hungry, only wanting to be there,*
> *Above the desiccated, cold bones of the crone*
> *In whose home you were born, were fledged.*
> *The vile hag who called herself your mother*
> *Now lies, as she always did.*
> *And you, issue of a woman so repulsive*
> *That the hair and nails—the only things down there,*
> *Deep in the earth,*
> > *that still attach to her gray skeleton,*
> *Her moldy frame of bones,*
> *Cardboard cartilage still pretending to cushion—*
> *Bearing only signs of dried brown blood*
> *And the curse that killed her kills you still.*
> *Damned you are.*

Your mother was an ugly and evil person.
Consider every kind, peaceful,
      beautiful remembrance of her —
And know the soul, spirit, psyche,
The essence of that loathsome horror
Is tortured in halls of hell,
Violated, orifices torn,
And more, the devil has more—
More ways to cause her pain
Than man's mind can conjure.
Even you.
Ravens gather at her grave
Because they like the feel.

Right now—this is right now—we do not contemplate.
We speak—our brains speak for us, in a way. It's all very rapid.
But it's not consciously considered, I think. It's just spontaneous.
And I think that you have to be able to look at what has been in order
to say something about the present moment. Even though poems come
spontaneously too. It's some sort of door into your unconscious, I guess.
                                —Ruth Stone

AFTER SEX

■

After sex
And the peremptory hug,
Like a transient uncle
Who hugs loosely,
Achieving a proper distance,
Pecks the cheek,
And retreats,
He migrated to the other side of the bed,
Not so slowly either,
Then hung on the precipice,
An arm under a head,
Legs curled under him.

I lay more fulfilled
Than used,
But more used
Than loved.

And wondered,
Is it men?
Or is it him, particularly?
Or is it women,
Or is it me, particularly?

THE BAFFLED BEAR

———■———

The baffled bear pricked his ears,
Then cocked his head like my chocolate Labrador, Sara,
When I hide a squeaky toy in my hand and tease her;
Naïve, inquisitive,
She, ten thousand years from her ancestors
Who'd have lunged and bit off my hand.

But my Lab, now trained—rendered obedient, docile—
Through millennia of breeding,
Accidental and purposeful both—
Acts the fool, chasing what detritus I have at hand,
And can throw across the yard:
A torn and muddy tennis ball.

The bear, his atavistic self momentarily subdued,
Repressed for an instant, His nature belied,
And he, unmeasured, unmanaged,
Suffering, or perhaps rejoicing,
That centuries of man's manipulation
Had not harnessed his *anima.*

And so, stopping there upon a remote untraversed trail—
This ursine hallowed ground—his own—
The bear waited,
Just a moment,
A deviant delay,
This one, surely this his only one ever: fatal

The type of delay, shorter than a blink
In an eternity of evolutionary change –
That Darwin only guessed,
Cumulatively, tamed some, and others made more wild.
The great bear's pause,
An action hardly symbol,

Indeed more profound,
Real, with consequences:
His genetic heritage becoming a cul-de-sac.
(Unlike that of my sweet Sara who, even now,
            nursed newborns at home)
He stands, ceasing to move toward me,

Abruptly so,
Indeed,
Lending me,
By his curiosity,
A moment to reach, raise my rifle,
And shoot him dead.

APOSTATE TREE

A tree,
There like a man,
Upside down,
Head in the ground
Legs in the air.

How untreelike;
I counseled it to do better.
A tree, I explained, in tones measured
So as not to offend,
Should be straight and narrowing,

Narrower and narrower still,
As it reaches that point where
I have to drop my head back,
Strain my neck to see its higher branches
When I stand close.

Tree, you have bifurcated
Yourself,
As if, in your youth, you could not
Decide which way to grow, or go,
In doing so, made yourself . . . unnatural.

Unlike Frost's traveler
You took both roads . . . indecisive,
Or boldly decisive, I'm not sure which.

Long you've stood, uncompromising,
Whilst Frost's traveler long he stood,
Finally taking the easier road,
Because few chose it.
But as for that the passing there . . . .

In your early years, a youth,
You chose to form a precarious fork,
Such as trees, some no doubt your ancestors,
Over thousands and thousands of years,
Have learned not to do.

Split, stood, stand yet,
Here firm, legs in the sky,
Boasting length and girth,
Stalwart symbols of one's awesome
Obligation to oneself.

I had written secret notebooks all during grade school
and high school, but I showed them to no one, neither parents
nor children. In fact, in grade school, learning a poem
was a punishment. One was made to stay after school
and learn a poem. I loved this punishment.
—Mon Van Duyn

A Tornado Hit the Neighboring Town

———■———

A tornado hit the neighboring town, the next town over,
You know, only miles, just a few, away,
Just down that road there, like they say
We are just down that road there.

We saw the pictures on the TV news:
Their houses rendered piles of pickup sticks,
Their auto repair shop moved across the highway
Into the cafeteria of their little kids' school.

There were dead, of course.
Not everyone escapes when the weather is that bad,
Or God that mad,
Or cold and hot air just collide, by mistake, I guess.

I saw the wavy lines on a multi-color map
Behind that nice, good-looking
Black weatherman I usually watch.
He must have gone to school for that.

He took a long stick, pointing to the gulf and the plains
And hills somewhere with nascent cheer
Struggling across his lips.
His usual benign smile now repressed.

Photos and film preceded his science,
His charts, all festooned with big arrows
And a big "H" for "high", I think,
And a big "L", must be for low.

That nice, black weatherman did well, I thought.
Attractive and clean and articulate,
Maybe the weatherman could be President.
He did well explaining how cold Canadian air

Shakes hands, then wrestles,
Argues with warm gulf breezes.
They are humid, those winds.
He could be my president.

The pointer-bearing café-au-lait man,
My choice for president,
Explained the origin of the deadly storm,
The carnage ignored.

That's his job, of course,
To explain how sinuous winds gather,
Get mean, conspire,
And go faster than a car can go.

Not to explain the dead.
That's someone else's job.
He explains winds.
Winds that conspire to destroy,

A great and devastating wind-cabal
Sky-evil,
Winds so mean they kill,
Like a racing car can kill,

More fearsome perhaps than a race car,
Because it is these winds
That leave cars folded up
Like they had been guided by a drunken fool

Over a guardrail or into an unforgiving tree,
Or forced by a suicidal pilot
Upon some other stolid elaboration
Of a human engineer or a reckless god.

He explains, pretends it is understood,
When it is as likely that capricious deities,
Artemis, Loki and Odin killed because they could;
Wrathful on our little neighbor. Just because.

Mr. Weatherman,
My new choice for president,
Ignored the dead.
Just like a real president,

Or some distracted academic,
Focused on the Big Picture,
The *casus belli*, not the result.
Facile theory trumping grisly dead.

Mr. Weatherman followed the dour anchorwoman
Who had read a script,
While her channel shared, showed
Their very own close-up photos of The Devastation.

They were exclusive photos,
Their cameraperson having gotten there first,
To tiptoe, turn, and pirouette
About and among random bricks,

Lumber, tin roofs bent,
The detritus as bewildered as its observers,
The "once was" of houses and stores,
All the work of a bored and powerful somebody

Who decided to sculpt for a moment,
Using just the materials at hand,
And not comprehending the power
At his command,

Went crazy, for only a moment, you see,
Then moved on to disassemble another town,
To flatten a wheatfield,
Or back to his home in the ether.

Anchorgal told us again that the photos were theirs.
That they had got there first.
The photos were theirs, exclusive.
Exclusive, I suppose, like some private club

A club that will not have me,
Except that I was not shunned by
This channel's Exclusive Club,
I was taken in and it shared its film with me.

And we saw in these photos:
- A barber pole lying in a cornfield.
- A stop sign in a tree.
- A limbless doll face down in a puddle.
- A coffin disinterred.

- The roof of the high school
  - Set nicely on the ground,
  - Snapped into an V,
  - An upside down teepee just set up
    by a nomad Indian.
- Books from their modest library
  - Rendered back to their individual pages,
  - Festooning every tree and vacant lot,
  - Though it is a small town
  - And the library was just a room
    in an old house.

An entrepreneurial sort, that TV channel,
Speeding white vans
Embellished with its Channel Number:
Three, or Five or Ten or Thirteen, I forget.

They own the film and photos,
The first of the ironically toppled steeples,
The more-ironic flattened funeral home,
Under the rubble, there are no photos of the missing.

The photos and film must have those
Little circled "Rs" or little "TMs" or something
To show you that it is theirs,
Not mine, nor yours, nor anybody else's,
But the property of the TV station.

"And now, here's our own Susan Smith
From Destructionville . . . with the first report . . . Susan . . ."
Even Susan is their own,
Like the film and photos, exclusive.

I wonder if they say the bronze weatherman belongs to them.
They must be proud of all the irony,
But they don't let on.
Their own young and pretty newsreader,

Rushes to stand there athwart a pretzelled girder,
Her station's logo and channel number
So prominently embroidered there
In her navy blue windbreaker.

Ah, the irony of Susan Smith,
Standing,
In front of the town's funeral home,
Destroyed,

Its rubble an indecipherable puzzle
Of building materials,
Disassembled,
For the next player to figure out.

Susan Smith, serious and mature,
Despite her lineless face,
And managed hair,
And perfect nails,

Nails on a white hand
Cradling the microphone
With the Three, or Five or Ten or Thirteen,
She is not breathless,

She should be breathless
In front of the dead and the dying people,
Before the dead and dying town.
She does not shout as she should, as they must have.

She *should* be stalwart and stern,
Leaving to us the tears and questions
About the terrible rending,

The tearing down.
Pretty and professional, disgustingly composed,
Standing there in her logoed windbreaker
In front of the funeral home.

Or former funeral home, that is,
In a town so unsurgically incised
That it cannot process its own dead.
An ignominy.

Unseen, unanswered, unexplained
Neither by the Anchorwoman,
The nice, black Weatherman
Nor Susan Smith.

I told you it was the next town over.
We used to go through there,
But we don't go there anymore,
No reason to.

Now we go around on the bypass.
We are small and they are small,
But we have a bypass, bypassing, I suppose,
Such as should be bypassed, as needs by bypassing.

Their town is a few minutes' drive,
But we don't go there, or through there.
We have a high school.
They have a high school.

A little kids' school,
A barber, library,
Stop signs, dolls,
And a funeral home.

They have all that stuff and so do we.
At least they did.
No reason for them to come here, or us there.
Now they don't have all that stuff.

We still do.
Now, they can come here and use our stuff.
And watch TV.
And see themselves as we do.

THE LIFE AND DEATH OF RUSSELL AND ME

———■———

A shard, a wrinkle, a hair:
    The substance of death = the superficiality of life.
A curve, a scar, a field:
    Your living of my life = my goal of your death.

But why do I still thrive on essence of air
        and the relatively of life?
Do you still try to gain?
The founding of death = what peripatetics will fear.

To cross the line, the bar, the bale
Would mean to never die.
The basis of death = the inability to live.

But we will try, will die, will rot
As we have done before.
For death will come to even philosophers who lie.
To themselves.

DROPPING DIRT

———■———

Throwing dirt in the grave:
Hallowed custom.
Jews do it, don't they?

Instead, they threw dirt in his face and, unoffended,
He thanked that he was vertical still, erect.
And walked away with a dirty face.

The dirt falls from the eyes as scales,
Crashes into the ground, dust.
On a body horizontal, the earth builds.

Six feet deep,
So heavy that if you awake and wish to leave,
You cannot.

A NEW TOOL

—■—

I used to judge a nation by how cool it was.
(Not Iceland, of course.)
But Kenya, Mozambique and Zimbabwe,
For their wildlife and wild life,
Germany and Italy, their cars and bars,
France, Gallic arrogance,
Mexico, beaches, food, and temples found.
Now I have a new cool tool.
"How many people want to get in
Compared with how many people want out?"
I need a new algorithm,
(And I don't mean Al Gore rhythm!)
New calculus.
America is cool.

I

A WOLF AND ME

———■———

On a winter day, I, without a sweater or coat,
Lost in the woods,
A wolf came and sat down next to me,
Offering his friendship, warmth and care.
Perhaps he offered his love, too.
Though I will never know.

It seemed he was the loving kind.
So thick was his coat
And so sweet his breath
That I could not smell death.
No foul odor of evil from his mouth,
Or body, or fur came to me.

Shivering, perhaps from cold,
Perhaps from a monstrous killer close,
My hands, feet, numb and blue,
The wolf weighed and wondered,
Then beckoned me to a small swale at the foot of a tree,
He reared and pushed me lightly to the ground.

Once down, he curled upon and around me,
His tail, though scrawny by measure to a fox,
Curled on me, already warming from his body,
As a slight snow dusted us both.
I awoke, warm, new snow around,
Him licking the frost from my hands, my face,

Then striding to the edge of a copse,
Growling and circling,
Low, slow,
Til I rose and followed
His determined steps,
Warm and afraid.

My grandfather, my grandmother,
Father and mother,
Books and movies, too
Told me fear,
I will be bitten, eaten,
Consumed.

Fear them.
Wolves, they instructed,
Eat little Russian children,
And would eat ours had we not
Learned their ways,
Exterminated them.

I walked to school
Fearing the wolf
Behind drugstore, supermarket,
The barber,
A fatal leap, fangs, fearsome,
From a neighbor's yard.

The wolf would not eat me,
Worse, he'd maul me, gnaw me,
Leave me half dead,
Limbless, eviscerated,
Still breathing,
Pitiless waif bleeding out his last.

They did not tell me about
Cars or Alcohol,
Or the men and women who abuse them.
They did not tell me about
Perfidy and Lies
And the men and women who use them.

Wolves are convenient.

MY MOM SAID NO

———■———

When I ate dirt, my mom said no,
And I did not care and ate on.

When I ran in the halls, the teachers said no,
And I did not care and ran on.

When my hands reached the top of her thigh,
The edge of her breast, she said no,

And I did not care and moved up,
Moved over and on.

When my wife said come home
I did not care and stayed on.

I deny the women who call me to order,
To account, to their construct of my proper behavior.

When God called,
I did not care,

And continued on still.
I carry on,

A life anchored to a feather,
Tethered to the fender of a speeding tank.

I'm especially interested in absence. Every photograph represents a moment that is no longer, passed, as well as ways of being that have disappeared. I've always been a little obsessed with the way photographs hold and create an object out of that moment. And I've often thought if you look at a photograph, if you really study the gestures and expressions that the people have in the photograph, you could see the rest of their lives, everything that's to come. I think my interest in photographs started after my mother died. I started looking at old photographs of her, trying to see if it was all there in the photographs, what was going to happen to her and to us and our lives. Is it here, or do I, as the poet, put it there? That's part of my fixation with photographs., Susan Sontag says the very act of taking a photograph is somewhat cruel and mean.

—Natasha Trethewey

SEEING AGAIN

I would like to know it is like
To recover my sight.
To see again!

But to know what it would be like
To see again,
I'd first have to be blind.

To recover my sight,
Would I not
First have to lose it?

He Looked Like My Grandfather

———■———

He was old when finally I looked.
Like my grandfather, maybe my uncle.
Me, not so slim,
But I'd seen only gray-tone photos,
All but one artlessly posed.
Every shot, grim and determined.

Puritan stock: proper, strict, contained.
Propriety posing, though
They were irreligious sorts,
Strangely gaunt approbation
Of liberal interpretations,
Of the bible, too.

Denouncing such as "the shackles of moderation",
"The bonds of relationships",
And, among the many, my favorite:
"The lawlessness of justice."
Mainly myth, I suppose.

Another, closer look:
He was older.
Yes, more like my grandfather, surely.
Small wonder that even at an early age
His face announced
Nascent asymmetry,

That while benign in the absolute,
Appeared as evil's onset,
Evil in his youth, perhaps true,
And in fact few doubted that.
Evil announces victory in,
Through, the countenance.

After years of trying,
Fully corrupted not only grandfather's soul,
But his visage, too.
Owning him all,
Satan gnawed
Great ravines in his face.

Evil cheered victory publicly, constantly,
Smiles and frowns alike
Announcing Mephisto's glory.
As I looked closer, this time suspiciously, at an angle,
(For I did not want him to stare back)
I reckoned him my father.

More photos of my father than of the others,
Still, even few,
Most from a distance, in groups, stiff and squinting,
So that divining personality was a precarious pursuit,
One likely to see saint where there was none;
Pol Pot or Stalin where there was piety.

Moving closer, still skeptical,
I saw the shapes, outlines of my forbears,
Jaw and lips, brow and eyes,
Slapped in place
By a hurried god,
Rushed to complete his work.

He aged as I moved closer,
And in eerie coincidence,
Looked back with my own intrusive stare,
For something: truth, lies,
Anything.
His expression immutable.

I regarded the furrows etched,
His face mine, until,
No room remaining for further insights,
My nose pressed full against the mirror.
His breath fogged my mirror,
And I breathed his own.

STILL IN LOVE WITH YOU

———■———

I liked when she pushed back her bangs,
She revealed her forehead,
Face full,
No disguise,
No half-face,
No lies.

Long bangs are device,
Subconscious hiding,
Dangling, dripping, descending.
(Except for eating, vision, breathing,
Stuff like that,
Her hair covered her entire face.)

Hair to her eyes, symbol,
Sign of shame.
A wall,
Working its wallness
To keep out, keep out, protect perhaps
Something.

A face too well hewn for bangs,
She needed to be nude,
A face nude sure,
But all nude
Not just face, but all.
All her.

Celebrate your face,
Love it as much as I love it.
Undress it,
Reveal you,
Disclose
Your beauty.

Her to her:
Face lined,
Chest flat,
Breasts different sizes,
Falling down,
Nipples too brown,
Insufficiently pink,
Nascent belly,
Wrinkles, circles,
Flabby arms,
Thick thighs, distorted:
Her to her.

Maybe others see her this way.
Everyone?
Except me.
I see correct, moist clay, smooth and brown,
More wet and smooth and brown than any clay
That honored hands that touched it.

Woman.
Women.
All woman.
All women?
Naturally hard
On themselves?

Magazines,
Television,
They say.
That's what people say.
But *they* are paradigms.
Truth-seeking through the souls of others.

Did Eve get stretch marks from Cain and Abel?
Did her ass fall after Seth?
Her thighs a cellulite canvas?
Violent, indigo maps of country roads,
Veiny mazes
Gathered at her ankles?

Where did Adam get his trophy wife?
For whom did he trade in Eve?
Where did Adam get a diamond tennis bracelet
For the first sinner, earth's only female,
When God had not yet invented gravity,
Had not contemplated the effects
       of its juggernaut on women?

I do not see brown nipples,
Drooped breasts,
When she pulls the straps over her arms.
Or if I see brown instead of pink, then I like brown.
She turns as she reaches behind her
To close her bra.

Still in bed,
Horizontal,
My head is propped for advantage.
Delicious.
Her loose blouse, oversized slacks, and those bangs,
Costume.

"You always want me to wear tight blouses,
Tight slacks, no bra, no makeup?
Everyone wears makeup!"
"Everyone doesn't do anything.
Darling, there is no 'always' nor 'never'.
Who are you dressing for, anyway?"

"I dress for everyone . . .
I mean . . . I dress for you."
Like a clumsy politician,
She groped for the right answer where there was none.
"No . . . I mean . . .
I dress for *me*," she signed at last.

"You had to think about it," I said.
"Why do you *always* want to remake me?"
"I don't *always* ever do anything.
Never. Absolutely.
No one ever does anything *always*," I said.
"Fuck you. I don't *fucking remake* you."

The fucking remaking of others,
And the fucking remaking of ourselves,
In time, in place, in motion,
A summary of millennia of philosophy,
Disembodied nymph, vain and callow youth,
Echo self-adoration.

"Understand
How you are.
Beautiful.
Unadorned.
Plain.
As it is."

"You
Patronize
Me.
This isn't poetry.
It is life.
You always have to be so deep."

She was not smiling.
I did not explain that there is never an always.
She never asked me
What I thought about her mind,
A beautiful mind, unadorned,
No mask there.

Once, she asked why
I would not want her
To feel comfortable with her.
Fair question.
I thought.
"I am selfish."

Isuppose for whatever reason I actively welcome being put down, something which perhaps goes back to my upbringing—that accusation of not being worthy which could be laid at one's door.
—Paul Muldoon

WINTER CAN BE PARDONED

———■———

Winter can be pardoned
For it know not what it does.
Its icy blasts the product of Free Will.
God, endowing this bleak season
With not only purpose and will, but means.

Bucolic scenes of five foot drifts,
Through the mind's mist,
Bitter and biting,
Pardon winter, and pardon its driven snows.
It knows not what it does.

Summer reasons.
Spring and Fall, seasons proclaiming
God's gift of conscious change,
But Winter has another call,
Unloosed by divine hand.

TOCK TICK

———■———

Tock, tick.
He raced in place,
The pace of grace.

Tock, tick.
He fought the feet,
That beat the street.

Tock, tick.
He scanned the plan
That ran the man.

Tock, tick.
A deadly lie,
Of blighted sky.

RANDOM

———■———

Random does not mean unimportant.
And you asking who started this
Is like a fireman asking who lit the match,
While the building is still ablaze.

No forensic fools trace accelerants,
While men in heavy coats and boots
Sweat and pant to finish the flames.
(Some die.)

Maybe you'll find out it was not robbery,
They just wanted him dead.
Shot in the head,
(His wallet's still here.)

Blacks gather and listen outside
White churches,
Huddle under the windows
Wide let the cool in, heat out,

Niggers can hear the Word.
But cannot learn to read or write,
You can hear Jesus,
But Jesus, what if they understand?

LEARNING RELEVANCE

He revealed his life as a search for the relevant.
He said, too, that
His life was abundant.

How do you tell a friend,
Tell anyone,
That relevance is in the life God delivered?

Do you know you are here by redemption?
You are relevant by grace alone?
You are relevant.

He graduated, still searching for relevance.
He said, too, that
His life was abundant,

Absent the sense that relevance commenced
With the first breathy cry,
Your creation, when sperm and egg shook hands.
.

He proclaimed his life a search for relevance,
His life abundant.
God's creatures irrelevant?

Darkness' Victor: man's acknowledgement
Of extrinsic worth:
A value proposition delivered by a fallen angel,

Performance measured,
Approval,
Blame and shame.

His millions cached,
He purchased Lucifer's lies:
His relevance was his abundance.

His sense begot nonsense.
Angels' decadence earned through man's descent,
Crossing paths perhaps with The Bloodied One,

Ascending, sent by God to,
Through, redemption,
To prove our relevance.

When he upon his deathly pallet lay,
When clarity would betray grace,
He asked the nature of himself.

From whence my relevance?
Too late!
Another presumptive angel.

Inside my empty bottle I was constructing a lighthouse
while all the others were making ships.
—Charles Simic

ART FROM LIFE

———■———

It was a surprise when you appeared,
There, smiling, without notice,

No triumphant fanfare,
Without knights and noblemen in escort,

No spear-bearing infantry in lockstep,
No flags unfurled,

Absent trumpets and messengers,
You were there.

Less smile than grin, I suppose,
And the grin itself asymmetrical,

Cheshire-catlike,
Without undisclosed purpose.

And now you are here.
No press release or advancemen,

Tanks or howitzers on Mayday parade,
No limousines with little flags on their front bumpers,

No men in black business suits jogging along.
You appeared: a vision, flourish-less.

Life from art, surely,
But more, art from life.

My whole work is to catch the word by surprise, sneaking up on language, sneaking up on the world as it lurks in words. I love the recesses of reason. That's a great place to set my mind at rest.
—Heather McHugh

You Catching Life's Woozle

———■———

Pooh and Piglet circled a copse,
Following paw-marks in the snow,
A certified pair of certified dopes.
Tracking the Whatever-It-Is
To Wherever-It-Goes.

Stupid and anxious, excitable and brave,
Like you, following life's paw-marks,
More innocent than depraved,
Chasing Whatever-The-Hell,
Seeking somehow to be ultimately saved
(In time, of course, to your grave.)

Milne's naïve little Piglet and Pooh,
Coming 'round the circle again,
Encounter their own footsteps anew,
Then taking the thicker trail as that of a new traveler,
Though each time they circle, their steps they redo.

Like you retracing your own self-worn trail:
Thinking that you're progressing,
While reciting your hackneyed tale
Of roads you've walked and lands explored
The insipid seeking its own Holy Grail.

You encounter "new" footsteps that are really your own:
And proclaim to the world that you are enlightened
By the seeds you have sown
Are left behind—gone on and flown—
While you trod your seeds back into the stone.

"This...whatever-it-was...has now been joined by another...
whatever-it-is... and they are now proceeding in company.
Would you mind coming with me, Piglet, in case they turn out
to be Hostile Animals?"

Your perilous cries are as hollow as you following
Your own repeated footsteps around the larches
With dreams and hopes
Trod thicker with each trip 'round.

And surrounded by Christopher Robins,
Seeking to set you right,
You'll not admit that you have been shallow,
Adhering to the rites of your own myopic sight,
Mind and mien woefully slight.

Christopher Robin explains to Pooh
To what extent he's been such a fool:
"Yes," said Winnie the Pooh.
"I see now," said Winnie the Pooh.
"I have been Foolish and Deluded," said he, "and I
*   am a Bear of No Brain at All."*

While you ignore your Christophers,
Walking your circular path,
Deeper and deeper,
Admiring how worn it's become,
Never noticing your own footprints,
        making the wear.

Two roads diverged in a yellow wood.
And be one traveler long you stood
And took the one most worn,
Following the host of former travelers who'd all
        gone before,
Except they were just you anyway.

Pooh, not too bothered by the revelation of his superficiality,
As Christopher Robin assures him
That he is the best bear in all the world.
 "*Am I?*" says Pooh hopefully, then cheering up,
Remembering it is almost lunch time, and goes home for it.

You are not the best bear in the world.
You forget that it is lunch time.
You will make more and more circles,
Pompously observing how better the trail becomes
With each completed turn,
And then starve.

YOU MUST SUFFER AND DIE LIKE THEM

On 911 the world changed.
Everything,
Everyone changed,
But me.
I the same,
Deserving their blame.

You must suffer and like them,
Like those that died, they said.
At least a little bit inside,
But better a lot.
Bleed, shed tears, vomit.
Care.

But I was the same,
No sorrow,
No joy,
No blame.
I just wore deep ruts in myself,
As always I had,

The twin towers burn and
Descend,
Tenants choking and screaming,
I do not shrug,
I do not cry,
I do not care.

My father died, then my mother,
In the order they usually do with one another.
I deserved their blame,
I did not change, my suffering already complete,
A lifetime full, I empty.
I do not cry for others

DIMENSIONING ORION

———■———

They asked me of Orion,
Don't you see it?
It's right there.
Right there in that galaxy.
Where?
There, over a little to the left,

That bright, distinctly-orange, star to the upper left
      of Orion's belt,
That's Betelgeuse.
One of Orion's shoulders.
The eleventh brightest star in the sky.
Three hundred and fifty light years from Earth.
That's 1,750,000,000,000,000 miles away, someone added.

I never saw Orion.

Perhaps it was not there.
A conspiracy of amateur astrologists
Gather in a clever cabal, gaze up,
Make meretricious claims.
Sky stuff makes fools of me and you,
Certainly me,

Because I never saw.
A gaggle of the over-enthusiastic,
No duplicitous natures,
Only convinced of forms
From nothing,

As I sometimes am,
Laying on my back,
Summer afternoon,
In the cloud sculpture above
I see Nixon and Agnew holding hands,
A Kudu speaking Urdu,
Splendid renderings of Angkor Wat,
Suryavaram II and Khmer Kings,
An empire of Buddhists, Hindus, closet-agnostics
Atop their cumulonimbus and altostratus thrones.

A Letter to My Red Maple

■

I suppose I should start out with an apology. After all, I have owned you for over twenty years and I have never given you any formal praise.

No recognition, no ceremonies, no awards, no trophies. Yes, I realize that I've never had to approach this relationship on a formal basis . . . and if I'd not have had to now, I'd likely never properly recognized your existence.

So, here you go: I'm sorry.

You've been in the front yard of this house for perhaps fifty years, planted by the gentleman from whom I bought this house, I suppose, but perhaps yours is a more feral story and you owe your existence to a bird or squirrel. Whichever, whatever, you are a good tree. I'm glad to have you around. There, I said it.

I hesitate so soon to qualify my recognition of your existence, nay, your worth, but I think we should agree that your contribution to our relationship has been circumscribed, aesthetics aside. Indeed, when I reckon the formal account, I accede somehow your contribution to me personally—and mankind, as well, I suppose—has been, how shall we say, *limited*.

You bear no fruit or nuts, as many do. Consider the millions upon millions of trees working diligently to give us oranges, lemons and grapefruit . . . walnuts, olives, pistachios, and almonds. Need I go on? Nothing like this from you, of course. And pecans, I forgot pecans. And think of all the berry trees that generate such wonderful output!

Nor will you ultimately yield your body for pulp or planks, like so many of your brethren. They're hewn apart in the din of sawmills to offer up quality studs and beams. Or eventually be shredded, boiled, mashed . . . to be formed into pressboard kitchen cabinets and such. Pine and oak go willingly for the cause of furniture . . . bedroom suites and divans and such. And important functional things like shipping pallets, telephone poles, and fence posts. These kinds of trees, well, they live on and on in our service. And how about musical instruments? And boats? Boy, those are real tree contributions!

Stradivari put spruce and willow to work. And guitars get their luxuriant, sonorous sounds from cedar, rosewood, and ebony. Baseball bats.

Plus, oaks and others render great service by offering shade for our houses and lawns. A real functional contribution there, don't you think? You offer shade, of course, but are too far from the house for us to ever conveniently gather beneath your leaves to take advantage of it. So that your shade, as a dividend, is a contribution that's really moot, as far as we are concerned.

I do acknowledge that you are cursed by being rooted. That can't be a good thing. If we decide we do not like you, we have lots of options: cut you down, trim you.

Worse, far worse, we can turn our heads and ignore you. We can even get you out of our lives by selling the whole place here . . . you with it, of course. Your choices, on the other hand are more, how shall we say, *limited*.

If an ill wind blows our way, we turn our backs, put up our hoods, or go inside. And rather than confront a blistering sun, we'll move to an air-conditioned room, or slather on sunblock and get a tan, or seek the expansive shade of an oak, perhaps.

Likewise, when the temperature drops to zero, we can fly to Cancun, St. Barth's or Maui (I will tell you about those places later); or just motor across town, sit before a friend's glowing fireplace. (I guess when I tell you about Cancun and Maui, I'll also tell you about what goes into a fireplace.)

Okay, you're right, enough of that mushy, negative stuff. I admit it. I look at you every day with love, admiration and respect. These days, in fact, I don't just look at you (several times a day), I *ponder* you, I consider you. That's different.

Do you remember when that ice storm caused those two big limbs to snap and crash to the ground? That time, I looked at you for a long time from the living room window and I cried.

I cried again a few days later, when I picked up the ends of those heavy branches and, wanting to find a way to stick them back on, I waited a long time, finally lugging them to the brush pile and there, at the bottom of the pasture, heaving them on.

Your wood was dense, I recall, the main branches heavy, and the smaller branches and remaining leaves grabbing the ground, fighting me the entire trip to ignominy.

As for you, I knew you'd rebound, grow back, and get that beautiful symmetry once again. You're tough, I know. But it's been nearly eight years now, and I can see that you are still a little crippled on your left side. That was a terrible storm. My friend Mike had a stroke the same day as that storm. He's not entirely better yet either, but he works hard at it, too.

I am looking to buy a place out of town . . . planning to move away. Of course, you'll have no choice to but to stay and do your best to impress the new owners. I will tell them exactly how I feel about you, okay? That I love you and that they have to honor you, silently, like I have. Whatever happens, don't worry. They'll look after you. Just keep standing there being beautiful and everything will turn out fine. Really.

I have an ongoing obsession with birds, landscape, the body—the
archetypal pairing of body and house—and I continue to think about
people being place bound, gender bound, or bound to the past. I return
always to the natural world for metaphor, and think I must have
been a biologist in some other life. In graduate school, I was accused of
attributing too much "nobility" to animals—and I still do! We are, as
Maxine Kumin says, not just "of" the world, but "in" it, and
I find all sorts of valuable, applicable lessons in paying very close
attention to animal life.

—Claudia Emerson

BLOOD LINES

———■———

They drew a line right here and said this is Libya.
And you, over there, you are Syria.
And you, by the way, are Turkey.
And, you sir, are Iraq.
And, way over there, you are Iran.

Lines of blood, they are called: Blood Lines,
Drawn by diplomats from far away,
With great armies and great navies.
Diplomats, no working-class accents, no middle-class tones,
In proper English, set out their plans
To damn the lives of Kurds, Baluch and Shia with a pen:
Blood Lines drawn in ink.

Kosovo, the Caucasus, the Congo,
Sketched on a lineless map by mindless men
With perfect nails, waistcoat and frock,
High white starched collar,
And solid gold Hampden pocket watch
(With fob artfully hung),
An obligatory hunting scene etched finely on the case.

The costume: striped pants and pearl tie pin,
All conspicuous, clarion billboards announcing,
Not so much intelligence, experience or wisdom,
But more, *birth.*
Entitlement is the proper child of proper birth,
And, subtly and catastrophically,
Inferred intelligence, experience and wisdom attach.

These Neville Chamberlains smoothly draw the feather pen,
Dip it in the well again, charging it to an (un)holy task,
The pen then drawn slowly across a parchment page,
Leaving a tribe, a clan, a holy place, a culture or civilization,
Divided.

Unnatural Saudi Arabia,
With armed Wahhabis holding Mecca and Medina
            as their own.
Or Cherokees off to arid Oklahoma, rendering, so to speak,
Unnecessary another line in the Carolinas.
Lines for Lebanon, Pakistan;
For Scots, Xhosa, Shona and Zulu, too,
Lines drawn by an arbitrary German, Brit and you.

A FIELD OF CLOVER

——■——

Climbing a low wooden fence,
I was in the field,
Knee deep in green,
Every inch small pink blossoms,
Or white ones,
I sat
Silently begging permission of the absent owner,
Motionless, still,
No breeze moved a leaf,
Clover and sky and bees and I.

Bees' faux randomness:
No general among them,
Only chaos,
Soldiers obeying orders
Etched in their cells through a million years,
Flying white to pink to white again,
On small mindless, magnificent missions.

The heroic still,
Deep their virtue, bodies and bones,
Those shot, trampled, lanced,
Whose blood fertilized,
Never rolled in its clover,
Or, if they did, in pain,
Of cannon, musket, the sword's evisceration.
And atop, clover.

The bees, ignorant of subterranean relic,
Soldiers' honor,
They work,
Mindlessly mindful,
Little journeys,
Flower and flower,
Warmed by the Flanders' sun,
All of it fungible.

Bees, identical,
Kneel to the flowers,
But for their white and pink hues,
The same.
Warriors' bones beneath,
Fleshless, anonymous,
No more honor in those of the patriot
Than those of the tyrant.

I reckoned flower and bee,
Until a clover finally trusted,
Spoke to me,
Strong and green with pink flower,
Yet bemoaning his fixedness.
And the bees flew through,
Pollinating, of course,

(I explained to the clover,
That I considered it fair exchange
For bee the nectar,
What other use than to feed the few foals
Set here in the late spring?)

But I wish to fly, the clover begged,
To be yellow and black,
Buzz a cryptic buzz
Own a random routine,
Assignment really,
Need to be busy at a task.
Means purpose.
Each day different,
On my own,
A wondrous flying fool.

I cautioned,
Routine it seems,
But each flight's an account kept,
No fabled flights of fancy,
These trips arranged, indeed dictated,
By choreographer unseen.
No bee is AWOL ever.

Then again tomorrow,
After a brief break
To shake the morning dew,
Then again to work.

What mighty crosses we bear, said the clover.
Me seeking flights,
If not of fancy, then of chore.
And the bees adorned,
Flaxen bands and black,
Knees with hunks of golden pollen,
Shuttle,
Disappear,
Return nectarless,
Begin
Again.
Where to they go?

Maybe below, to commune with hero's bones,
From whom you suck
What remains,
To feed your greenness,
Then for the foals
Who soon be upon you.

Predestined are we not?
Me to roots,
Him to wings,
Bones beneath to feed us both,
All factious and fated the same?
Ah, but should you be the pollen?
The nectar?
The patriot?
The tyrant?
Curse them
For not being the other?

Or curse that oak,
Holding his branches firm for nesting birds,
To adorn, without wail or whine?
While you grow hardy green
And nod to the sun and breeze.

You clover buzz, pollen is nectar,
The oak bears small pink flowers,
The bee sits in a fine green place.

As for me, I wish to be all
And none of you, too.
Envy creeps a green,
Pride levers,
Works the locks,
So I pause,
Recall thorns, a rock rolled away,
To make this field, clover, bee,
The souls of men whose bones below you lay.

Either move or be moved.
—W.S, Merwin

GROWING BACK

———■———

The grass grew here once.
Not a green carpet like the lawns in town,
But wiry and tufted and long,
So that it brushed your shins like that grass there.

This spot was no different
From that one over there. Or over there.
And not so long ago.
You would remember it, if you were here.

It could grow back again.
I think it could grow back again.
It'd probably take a long time.
No, I don't know how long.

A long time.
We'd have to stop coming here.
Walking on it.
Looking at it, I guess.

Like a pot of water left to boil,
Leave it alone.
That'd be hard, to stop coming here.
But it'd grow back, I think.

STREETS OF HELL

———■———

The streets of hell are paved with gold,
Gold from souls that sold what mattered,
Bartered the material,
Dealt the ethereal peace of God's endow,

Now chattel of evil,
They crossed Styx and Archeron—
(Free passage the deal),
Not gleaning the merest notion that Charon's goal

An ocean of fire and pride, easy in.
As heaven,
Free, you see,
Renounce your sin,

Take the bloodied crown to heart,
And float with Peter,
Instead of Charon, at the wheel,
The bloodied pierced hands and feet.

A simple start.
Your burden owned by another.
But the evil surely knows:
Streets paved with gold.

A CASKET, A BASKET

A casket,
A basket of hope dashed,
Smashed,
Faith cashiered like a delinquent.

A teen, his car tumbles like a toy across a ditch,
No hope for his body,
Crushed as the
Instrument of death itself.

A middle-aged mother for whom cancer
Is the final sentence.
Breasts removed, but no malignant might,
A juggernaut against the widowers' wails.

Dreams denied,
They cease.

Old man, but alive by law,
His family has faith,
For here or beyond,
They do not even know.

But faith fails.
Caskets descend into spaces
Carved into hard winter dirt,
Tears descend, too.

TALK, TALK, TALK

———■———

Talk, talk, talk,
Walk, walk, walk,
A reader not knowing where to
Go up you must actually climb a stair.
Narrow?
Snakily sinuous?
Ground us.
Grass green?
Hills? Roil or roll?
Bob and Mary,
Their jabbering hangs.
Where are they're going?
Nice job on their mood, their motivation,
I'm clued, they're on vacation.
But give us some sense of their direction.
And don't they fucking *care* about anything?

GETTING EXERCISE

———■———

Isaac Newton was wrong:
      it was a peach what fell from that tree.
(Horace and MacLeish knew that.)
It fell from Kankakee,
Blizzards of fruit, crashed
On an Illinois town,
Bound as I,
That the conqueror silent sleeps,
When invincible hand cleared
      the rude and thoughtless sky bridge.
Next year at this time, you cannot younger be
Oy vey!
Unless you eat of the giving tree,
Then die a coward dog
And see that peach is fruit, color
And odor.
Can it be three?
Arlo's and Carlos' and Isaac's independent ideas ignite
An argument:
Ah, gravity.
It is a serious though inexplicable force,
A grave situation where on the hole the digger triumphs.

SINGLES

———◼———

She.
Her.
One husband.
One child.

One house.
One job.
One car.
One cell phone.

One lover.
Units.
Linear,
Lateral.

Child at home?
Job at home?
Lover in the house?
The lover in her?

The choices are simple, ma'am.
Look in the bin:
There is only one of each.
The choices are simple until the bin empties.

The difference between the right word
and the almost right word is the
difference between lightning
and a lightning bug.
—Mark Twain

ONE SUNNY DAY

———■———

Sunny day,
A hostile cloud flies,
Tries to say hi,
I welcome the visit,
Embrace its quaint hello,
Ignorant of intents to dupe,
Fool me,
Lead me on.
Belligerent vapor,
I know your ways,
Tempt smiles from men's lips,
Educe pleasure songs,
Then attack,
Pillage, torture, and rape.
I, now wise, descry your disguise:
You are water,
Formed into white fluffy pillows,
A benign demon,
Intentions hid.

Poetry is not a turning loose of emotion,
but an escape from emotion; it is not the expression of personality,
but an escape from personality. But, of course, only those who have
personality and emotions know what it means
to want to escape from these things.
—T.S. Eliot

I WISH PEOPLE HAD TAILS LIKE DOGS

———■———

I wish people had tails like dogs,
So I can know what they think.

There is a cagey canine out there somewhere,
Able to disguise his feelings.

But he'd be rare.
I'd dare you to find such a dog.

Find a dog who can hold his tail when he's happy.
One who'll not growl or howl or snarl.

That dog whose fears and joys
Are not on his lips, the hair on his back,

And betraying tail,
Mood triggers motion, iconic emotion.

People are stoic, stone-faced,
They perjure and pretend,

Tend to tell you how to steer,
How to be.

People tell you they love you,
Tell you they are happy

When they are down,
Tell you they are down when they're not.

Act, emote,
Shed tears of despair,

While their minds conjure,
Measure your response, calculate.

If people had tails like dogs,
They'd see you on the street,

And instead of acting cool,
They'd sidle, slobber and wag their tails.

And if a person with a tail was afraid of you,
Or just didn't like you, boy, you'd know.

If you had a tail, it would keep you honest.
And my charades would be ended, too.

Mostly, I'd wag my tail, vigorously,
Like a puppy.

An Upset Normal Woman in Time

———■———

Upset, but rational.
She was crazy,
But, well,
Her own sort of hell.

Ten thousand confusions;
Anxieties crammed into a small smooth fist.
First aware:
The possibility of nonbeing.

Find the spot empty was full,
Self refracted to love,
Impatient to that place,
Slough the real, the rest, the race.

Glory in the dualism of now-conscience,
Memory passed.
Wink, whim and whisper last
Beyond the despair of knowing?

A moment, you brief?
No decades, nor years,
Bending light and time,
Somatic senses.

Attenuated cherish.
Reveries perish,
Time rots.
It's must be short.

Place, as time *cum* motion, dear,
Else how to revere?
Priceless only because it can go.
But to know a year?

Decades slow?
Her ephemeral moments are hers,
Belonging. Possessions. Ownership.
In ways not just deferred,

But, you guessed, repressed.
Bad?
Good?
Evil?
No: normal.

CERTIFICATE DEMANDED

——■——

Okay, so if the Treasurer's Office agrees,
And the Dean says so,
That I paid full tuition to the College of Life,
And the Registrar's Office says okay,
That I completed all the courses,
Never anything worse than a D-.
And I have been practicing my course of study for decades,
Why can't you send me my hard-earned degree?
I returned a self-addressed stamped envelope.
I have here a nice document frame,
Matted and with non-glare glass,
Black with a thin gold stripe,
Like in a dentist's office,
Or the wall of a personal injury attorney.

Shouting credibility.
I await said diploma.

You do not respond to my repeated requests,
Are you still open?
Still educating the young?
Still hurting hearts, rending minds?
Ah, that's the stuff; great college you are!
Please, kind sir, send me my fucking diploma,
Or I will sue your ass so bad
          you will not know which way to turn.

You see, I learn.

SUCH GRUDGE

———■———

Jesus, you held such grudges.
If I kept you up late reading,
As I always did,
You'd put salt in my orange juice.
It sounds cute now,
But it's not funny,
Wasn't then.
Pathological then.
You're not much changed, now are you?
Remember if you got fouled
In one of our backyard basketball games,
How you'd just get quiet?
Scary, it was, that's what it was, scary.
When I think about it now,
I mean it was just backyard stuff,
All friends,
And you'd come back and smash one of us
As some sort of penance or punishment
Or whatever it is to you.
You put salt in the basketball game,
Sugar in my bed, my gas tank, my ears.
You are not my sister anymore you hear me?
And you are not my lover any more, either.

I *believe that one day the distance
between myself and God will disappear.*
—Franz Wright

LIMBO: THE FALL

——■——

The thoughts of what will come too soon
And what is too soon past
Define the way we now exist:
This state will always last.

Will always last until it ends,
Then Stevens' blackbirds fly;
And we, more quickly than we guessed,
Will share Socratic eye.

But now we pace the fallen leaves
Which blacken under tread,
And like us, fallen from the branch,
Will fall with Cold, be dead.

But Fall, they say, is to be lived
(while living watching walls)
And waiting for the leaf to pale
(And when it pales, it falls.)

Its falling is an endless time,
As our fall soon will be,
And when It comes, we must look back
To see our one-branched tree.

Its single branch we will not know
Until it is too late;
To think of how we wasted Spring
And sealed late Summer's fate.

Although we walk below that tree,
We now are in our Fall;
Sent back and forth, and here and there,
But always down, withal.

And Falling from the first we know
That promised leaves we pass,
We know our final resting place:
Sere upon the grass.

In Fall there is no up or down,
There is no now, no past.
There is no ground, no gravity,
For now the die are cast.

And tumbling down toward other leaves,
By other leaves we've passed;
There is no ground to cease our fall,
This State will always last.

REDEMPTION

———■———

I prophesize my death,
Brilliant am I.
Soon to leave this vaunted orb,
Rise into the sky.
If judgment pales above,
I a sinner go
To fires, pestilence, pain?
Eternity, you say?
Faith in blood, wet then dried brown and caky,
   flaky in the dirt.
Scars on hands and feet.
A might grace forgives,
And I my savior meet.

MY MEMORY HAS TRANSFORMED YOU
INTO A CLASSIC BEAUTY

———■———

My mind is as any Alzheimer's-afflicted craftsman:
Skills still sharp.
The musician's harp rings: notes never before played,
    not even written.
Vibrating strings of creativity: undecayed by brain pathology.
Not remembering is my gift, not my curse.

As treasure yielding liberation,
        no chains of truth bind my mind.
I am enabled, empowered by my flaw,
To re-create you as awful crone or classic beauty.
So I choose that you transform to beauty,
As is (or would be) my (crippled) mind's desire.

Today, this is the (only) way I can love you.
Archetypal charms and grace transcend
Again.
Helen stands beside you;
Gawky and plain how she is.

They call my new memory a dis-ability,
But I feel no dis.
Or if dis-ability it is, then, fine.
I recall only that
My mind now insists you are.

To pay attention, this is our endless and proper work.
—Mary Oliver

EMMETT TILL WAS A CATHOLIC

Emmett Till a Catholic.
Irish. Ultranationalist. Republican freedom fighter.
O'Till, McTill.
And still we'll not
Take honor from the
Mississippi Orange loyalist,
Reckoning that whistling at a whitewoman
In Mississippi
And hurling
Are each condemnable sins,
Unpardonable,
Though the RUC, Judge , Jury British Police,
Balaclava-hooded
Executioners
Like their Mississippi counterparts.
A dead Mick dying in the Bogside,
A dead nigger in Chicago,
Souls and blood mixing in misery
On a hot Leflore county summer,
A cool Belfast summer,
Tallahatchie River and Falls Road,
Icons of an eternity of man's hatred for man.
Man himself despised by man himself.

SERIOUS RADIO

———■———

I'm done with giddy radio, with silly radio.
I got a gift:
Serious radio, serious satellite stuff.
Perfect, I thought.
How I will adore the *gravitas* of my new radio.

No sprightly marches;
No Bobby McFerrin, no Debbie Boone;
Just dismal dirges, sniveling DJs,
Johnny Cash (from his prison collection),
NPR reports on Diana of Wales.

MY DAUGHTER WENT TO BORE-DINK SCHOOL

—■—

My Daughter went to bore-dink school,
So said my Russian immigrant father,
A latter day H*Y*M*A*N K*A*P*L*A*N.

He could not conceive, not believe,
That one takes a fortune,
Sending it off, like her, to a distant place,
With Georgian (or Gothic, maybe) castles,
Amid literal green pastures,
And expects in return an adult,
A worker with strong hands, strong shoulders, strong back,
A person who could possibly understand Buchenwald,
Or Bergen Belsen, Dachau, Treblinka,
Babi Yar, Nanking or Srebrenica.

LONG DIVISION

———■———

I divided society:
Black, white,
Tall, short,
Smart, dumb,
Rich, poor,
Pretty, ugly,
Fat, think.
Half of them I deplore.
Then, they asked me to divide myself.

THE RHYME IS THE CRIME

———■———

Long word, thick with mascara,
Rouge and crimson lipstick,
All made up for the novel, essay and ode,
Pomp for the poem,
Bullying past more worthy words
By force of syllable, sound.
Not its nature, not what it *is*,
That qualifies a word,
Makes us reach,
Take it from the shelf of words,
Consider it, work it into the stew.
Work and worker ruminate.
Our arm stretches
And our fingers grasp words of glory,
Flamboyant Zouaves,
Rococo popinjays,
And baroque furbelows.
Callow braggarts beg,
"How do I sound?"
"How do I look?"
Shout to the heavens,
"Look at me, see how long I am
And what difficult letters I employ!"
They puff little literary chests
Tout tone and length,

Shout elaborations and complications,
Tricking us with superficial charm.
They overlook both meat and marrow.
Do tone and length make the word the measure of itself?
It is something else, no?
No?
Essence.
Marrow.
Selfless selfness.

"I have . . .
    Meaning.
    Soul.
    Purpose.
    Direction!"
Shouts the short word.

But we discriminate, worthy word.
Seek syllables,
Vainly lever length,
Our education and wisdom
Wreak and reek.

"Respect me!"
"Si se puede!"

I would agree that it's the medium or it's the kind of literature where you have a most intimate and direct relationship between writer and reader. You don't come at the reader with ideas and opinions, you try to bring a whole person into the poem, and you have a sense . . . when it works, you have a sense of immediate contact with another person.

—Carl Dennis

HENOTHEISM

———■———

I have been with you, about you,
You in me,
And me in you,
You not obeyed or obeying.
God, the Father,
No, God the Mother.
Mother of God!
God is coming and boy is she pissed!
God, She was slow to anger like
The other women in my life.
But, God was a woman not to be denied
Or crucified.
She did not call twice.
God does not supplicate.

I KNOW NOT WHAT I KNEW

———■———

I know not what knew,
Nor never I did.
The bridge of conscious memory flew
To a synapse that lapsed.
That could rid a man of a thought
So fast!
Who knew?

"When did you first forget
That you never knew this fact?" the lawyer asked.
My brain could think, shrink,
Hide from the burden of
A store of love.
Of lore,
Passing Jung to another realm.

T*he more constraints one imposes,*
The more one frees oneself of the chains . . .
The arbitrariness of the constraint only
Serves to obtain precision of execution.
      —Igor Stravinsky

PACING TIME

No calendar have I.
Consigned to a young man's grave,
I will say that I gave time
To know man,
And from no man
Borrowed a tiny minute.

A sin it is to take that time,
Lost in pages of dates,
And while away hours
Of ours and yours,
No course set for a youthful debt
Of borrowed time.

SCIENCE FAILS AGAIN

——■——

No scientist can tell why a bird sings.
They try,
To establish territory, a story that's nearly so,
I know,
A man must have space,
A place, to grow,
It's surely so for a crow.
(Though crows less sing than offer a croak.)
Move over, I need my space.
I was here first, get off my case,
The bird warbles.

To find a mate, a boy or girl
With whom to have a winsome whirl,
To furl wings (and other parts),
On cold nights to curl before the fire,
A lass or lad of similar kind,
From a lofty perch he sings to find
A cute feathered friend,
And in the end,
To be laid,
The eggs, that is,
Hatching. Fledglings devour bugs and such
'Til they are old enough to leave home,
And begin this thing again.

READERS' NOTES

—■—

The Bombing of **Dresden** by the British Royal Air Force and U.S. Air Force in February 1945, twelve weeks before the surrender of the Nazi Germany, is one of the most controversial Allied actions of the Second World War. 1,300 heavy bombers dropped 4,000 tons of high-explosive bombs and incendiary devices, laying waste to 13 square miles of the baroque capital of the German state of Saxony, causing a firestorm that consumed the city centre. Civilian casualties were between 30,000 and 40,000. A 1953 U.S. Air Force study defended the operation as the justified bombing of military and industrial targets: major rail transportation and communication center, housing 110 factories and 50,000 workers in support of the German war effort. Contrarily, many have argued that not all of the communications infrastructure, such as the bridges, were in fact targeted, nor were the extensive industrial areas outside the city centre. It has been argued that Dresden was a great cultural landmark with little military significance; the attacks were indiscriminate area bombing, and not proportional for the military goal, purposefully causing maximum civilian death and terror.

—■—

The **Shankill** Road leads through a Protestant working-class area of Belfast, Northern Ireland. Today, the area is known for its murals depicting Ulster loyalist sympathies. During The Troubles, Shankill and its residents were subjected to bombings and shootings by Irish republican paramilitary forces, the most notable of which is 'Shankill Bomb'. On October 1993, a bomb exploded in Frizzells Fish Shop.

The IRA claimed they were targeting a Loyalist meeting above the fish shop when the bomb exploded as it was being planted. Nine people were killed in addition to one of the bombers. The Shankill was also notorious for the terrorist actions of various Loyalist forces, such as those of the Shankill Butchers led by Lenny Murphy.

———■———

Bertrand **Russell** was a British philosopher, logician, mathematician, historian, social reformist, and pacifist. Russell led the British "revolt against Idealism" in the early 1900s and is considered one of the founders of analytic philosophy. His works have had a considerable influence on logic, mathematics, set theory, linguistics and analytic philosophy. He was a prominent anti-war activist, championed free trade and anti-imperialism. Russell was imprisoned for his pacifist activism during World War I, campaigned against Adolf Hitler; for nuclear disarmament; criticized Soviet totalitarianism and the United States of America's involvement in the Vietnam War.

———■———

Filling the grave is arguably the most striking part of a Jewish funeral, surely the most painful, and perhaps the most healing. Depending on the local custom, while the coffin is lowered into the earth, or just prior to filling the grave, the rabbi or cantor recites scripture, then hands the principal mourners a trowel or simply gestures for them to pick up a shovel placed beside a pile of newly dug earth. Children, parents, siblings, and spouse come forward, taking turns **dropping a little of the dirt** onto the coffin.

In November 2004, student Kenton Joel Carnegie was in Canada, walking alone near a remote camp owned by a mining exploration company, when it is *believed* that he was killed by **wolves**. The investigation was inconclusive, but some thought that wolves in the area had been attracted to a garbage indeed wolf-related, *it was the first documented case in the wild of healthy wolves killing a human in North America since the late 19th Century.*

———■———

A **woozle** is a fictional creature in the Winnie the Pooh stories. No woozle illustrations appear in A. A. Milne's original stories, but it might look something like a weasel. Woozles, which frequently travel with Wizzles, are first mentioned in a Pooh storybook when Pooh Bear and Piglet attempt to capture a woozle, but it is later revealed that the two woozles and two wizzles were really the footprints made in the snow by the duo, an error pointed out by Christopher Robin as he watches the two go round and round the larch spinney at least five times.

———■———

Colonialism naturally entailed administration of boundaries which European powers had drawn between the territories they carved out for themselves. Maps and borders imposed by colonial powers, viewed as external impositions, were subjects of understandable hostility. Some say that colonialist cartography placed various regions at a disadvantage in the global order. Post-colonial states have been insecure entities, yet the colonial maps have survived as the delineators of boundaries between these states. All this happened despite the arbitrary nature of much colonial map-making. Conferences and diplomatic maneuverings in distant European capitals often were responsible for national boundaries, lines drawn to deal with tensions among the colonizing powers rather than addressing genuine local issues. Colonial officials created political borders based on the claims of rival European powers and the whims of colonial administrators, who preferred using physical boundaries or lines of latitude and longitude to construct the borders of their colonial possessions. This boundary-making failed to take previous settlement patterns into consideration and therefore created political systems that lumped and split diverse pre-colonial communities. The lack of social homogeneity, in turn, promoted civil violence in a number of post-colonial settings, hence the term **bloodlines**.

———————■———————

Emmett Till, an African-American boy from Chicago, was murdered for whistling at a white woman, at the age of 14 in Money, Mississippi, a small town in the state's Delta region. The murder was one of the leading events in the nascent American Civil Rights Movement. The suspects were acquitted, later admit to the crime. Till's mother insisted on a public funeral, with an open casket to show the world the brutality of the killing. Till was beaten, his eye had been gouged out, before he was shot through the head and thrown into the Tallahatchie River tied, with barbed wire, to a 70-pound cotton gin fan. His body was in the river for three days before it was discovered by fishermen.

In 1970, the Falls Road was the scene of the Falls Curfew. In response to a gun and grenade attack, by the Provisional IRA, 3,000 British army troops sealed off the streets around the Falls Road, home to 10,000, flooding the area with soldiers in an attempt to recover IRA weapons. After an all-day gun battle, ninety rifles were recovered and over the course of the weekend, four Catholic civilians were killed by the soldiers. This event is widely regarded as the end of the British army's "honeymoon" period with the Irish nationalist community in Northern Ireland. For the following thirty years the British Army and maintained a substantial presence on the Falls Road, An area that saw some of the worst violence of the Troubles. The Battle of the Bogside was a communal riot between residents of the Bogside area of Northern Ireland's Derry city and the Royal Ulster Constabulary. Rioting continued for three days in the Bogside. The riot, which sparked widespread violence elsewhere in Northern Ireland, is commonly seen as one of the first major confrontations in the conflict known as The Troubles, which eventually claimed nearly 4,000 lives.

———■———

Hyman Kaplan, or **H*Y*M*A*N K*A*P*L*A*N** as he signs his name, is a character in a series of immensely popular, humorous stories by Leo Rosten, originally published in *The New Yorker* in the 1930s.

———■———

Henotheism is worshiping a single god while accepting the existence or possible existence of other deities.

———■———

Rene Descartes noted that the testimony of the senses with regard to any particular judgement about the external world can be wrong. Things are not always as they seem at first glance. He argues that we should never wholly trust the truth that we perceive. In ordinary life, of course, we adjust for mistaken perceptions by reference to correct perceptions. But since we cannot be sure at first which cases are verifiable, true and real...and which are not, it is possible to doubt any apparent sensory knowledge.

CPSIA information can be obtained at www.ICGtesting.com
Printed in the USA
241176LV00001B/3/P